Celebrate
Islamic Festivals

Series editor: Jan Thompson

Khadijah Knight

Heinemann
LIBRARY

© 1997 Reed Educational & Professional Publishing
Published by Heinemann Library,
an imprint of Reed Educational & Professional
Publishing,
100 North LaSalle, Suite 1010 Chicago, IL 60602
Customer Service Telephone: 88-454-2279
World Wide Web: www.heinemannlibrary.com

Designed by Sue Clarke
Illustrated by Jeff Edwards
Color reproduction by Track QSP
Printed in Hong Kong by
Wing King Tong Company Limited.

02 01 00
10 9 8 7 6 5 4 3 2

Library of Congress Cataloging-in-Publicatio
Data
Knight, Khadijah.
    Islamic Festivals / Khadijah Knight.
        p.   cm. -- (Celebrate!)
    Includes index.
    Summary: Introduces the festivals celebrated in
    the Islamic faith.
    ISBN 0-431-06964-6 (lib. bdg.)
    1. Festivals--Islamic countries--Juvenile
literature.   2. Rites and ceremonies--Islamic
countries--Juvenile literature.   [1. Fasts and
feasts--Islam.   2. Islam--Customs and practices.
3. Muslims--Social life and customs.]   I. Title.
II. Series.
BP186.K56   1997
394.26917'671--dc21   96-5325
                                                    CIP
                                                    A

Acknowledgments
The author would like to thank the following people for
helping with this book by having their pictures taken or by
giving their views on the writing:

Hussain Khan and his family; Fatimah Meyzin and her family;
Ibrahim Muhammad and his family; Muhsin J Kilby and his
family; members of the most honourable Naqshbandi Sufi
order.

The Publishers would like to thank the following for
permission to reproduce photographs.

Muhsin Jak Kilby: p. 4, p. 5; C S Nielsen/Bruce Coleman
Limited: p. 6; Muhsin Jak Kilby: p. 8, p. 9, p. 10; Trip: p. 11;
Muhsin Jak Kilby: p. 12, p. 13, p. 14, p. 15, p. 16; Sayyed Jaffer
al-Bassam: p. 17; R. Dalmaine/Barnaby's Picture Library: p. 18;
Gobet-APF: p..19; Muhsin Jak Kilby: p. 20, p. 21, p. 22, p. 24, p.
25, p. 26, p. 27, p. 28, p. 29; Peter Sanders: p. 30; Trip/A Di
Nola: p. 31; Muhsin Jak Kilby: p. 32; Circa Photo Library: p.
33; Muhsin Jak Kilby: p. 34; Muslim Aid, Islamic Relief, Human
Appeal International: p. 35; Muhsin Jak Kilby: p. 36, p. 38; Trip:
p. 39; Muhsin Jak Kilby: p. 40, p. 41, p. 42, p. 43

Cover photograph is reproduced with the permission of
Peter Sanders.

Our thanks to Denise Cush, David McCarthy, and Elizabe
Bladon for their comments in the preparation of this boo

**Whenever Muslims mention the Prophet
Muhammad, the words "peace and blessings of
Allah upon him" are said in Arabic. This is shown
in this book by the letters PBUH. Whenever
prophets and the twelve Shi'ah Imams are
mentioned, Muslims say "peace be upon him."
This is shown in this book by the letters PUH.**

Contents

Introduction

Every Friday Hussain, his parents, and his sister Maryam go to the mosque, where everyone recites the Koran and Allah's beautiful names.

Hussain and Fatimah are both **Muslims**. Hussain is eleven and Fatimah is eight. Fatimah has two older brothers, Mehmet and Mahmoud. Their family works hard to help Muslims in the United States keep their Islamic traditions.

Who are the Muslims?

Anyone, anywhere, whatever their race or nationality, can be or become a Muslim, anytime during his or her life. A Muslim is someone who believes that there is only one God—**Allah**, the Creator of everything. Muslims believe that Allah sent messengers and books to teach people how to live a good life. Muslims try to be at peace with themselves and with all of Allah's creatures and creation by following the principles of Islam. They believe that these were revealed to Allah's final messenger, the Prophet Muhammad **PBUH**. These principles are only part of what makes a person a good Muslim.

What is Islam?

Islam is the way people live by following Allah's guidance. Islam is "the natural way of life" for more than a billion people in the world today. Islam teaches that everything that people do is written down by angels and will be judged by Allah on the Day of Judgment. Allah will decide whether people will be rewarded for their good deeds or punished for their bad actions. Muslims believe that Allah is just and merciful.

The two main branches of Islam are **Sunni** and **Shi'ah**. All Muslims follow the teachings of the **Koran**—Allah's revealed book—and the example of the Prophet Muhammad PBUH.

The principles of Islam

Shahadah—the statement of belief that "There is no god except Allah and Muhammad is the Messenger of Allah."

Salah—worship of Allah. Muslims have to recite salah five times a day in Arabic.

Sawm—fasting during daylight hours in the month of Ramadan.

Zakah—making payment of 2.5 percent welfare tax on wealth.

Hajj—going on a pilgrimage.

Fatimah wears a headscarf not only for salah, but all the time. Hussain keeps his head covered, too, either with a hat or a turban.

Festivals

Lunar phases

By watching for the new moon and by observing each of its phases, Muslims have a calendar in the sky.

All **Muslims** use a lunar calendar. It is called the **Hijrah** calendar, and began when the Prophet Muhammad PBUH moved to **Madinah**. The word *Hijrah* means "emigration" or "departure." Each month starts by seeing the new moon. There are 12 months in the Islamic calendar. The Islamic lunar year is about eleven days shorter than the 365-day fixed calendar. Each year, each Islamic month starts eleven days earlier than the year before. So, there are no fixed winter, spring, or fall festivals in Islam.

"It is not permitted to the sun to catch up the moon, nor can the night outstrip the day: each just swims along in its own orbit according to the law." (**Koran** 36:40)

"The number of months in the sight of **Allah** is 12 in a year—so ordained by Him the day He created the heavens and the earth." (Koran 9:36)

he sun

he sun has a useful part to play
 understanding the Muslim day.
r Muslims, each day ends and
other begins at sunset. When
e sun sets on Thursday, Friday
gins. Even if there were no
ocks, Muslims could work out
e time to offer **salah** five times
day from the position of the sun
 the sky. They start very early
th the **fajr**, the dawn salah,
fore the sun has come up.

Times to offer Salah

Salat-ul-Fajr is between the first
light of dawn and sunrise.
Salat-ul-Zuhr is after midday.
Salat-ul-Asr is the mid-afternoon.
Salat-ul-Maghrib is sunset.
Salat-ul-Isha starts an hour and a
half after sunset.

This Islamic
calendar wheel
shows some
Islamic events
in the lunar
year, which
begins with the
month of
Muharram.

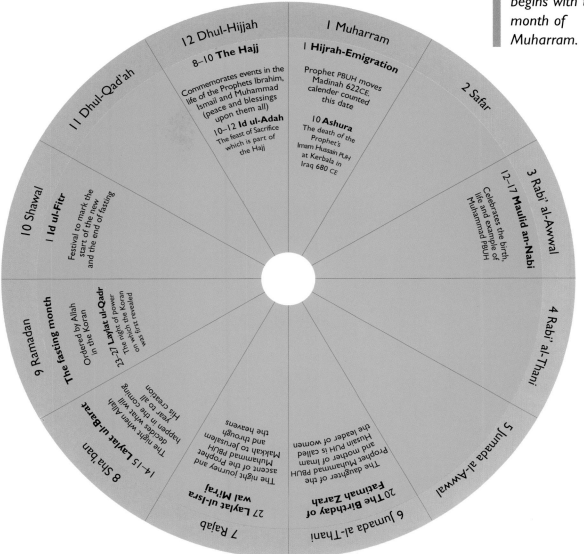

12 Dhul-Hijjah

8–10 **The Hajj**
Commemorates events in the
life of the Prophets Ibrahim,
Ismail and Muhammad
(peace and blessings
upon them all)
10–12 **Id ul-Adah**
The feast of Sacrifice
which is part of
the Hajj

1 Muharram

1 **Hijrah-Emigration**
Prophet PBUH moves
Madinah 622CE.
calender counted
this date

10 **Ashura**
The death of the
Prophet's
Imam Hussain PUH
at Kerbala in
Iraq 680 CE

2 Safar

3 Rabi' al-Awwal
12–17 **Maulid an-Nabi**
Celebrates the birth,
life and example of
Muhammad PBUH

11 Dhul-Qad'ah

10 Shawal
1 **Id ul-Fitr**
Festival to mark the
start of the new
and the end of fasting

4 Rabi' al-Thani

9 Ramadan
The fasting month
Ordered by Allah
in the Koran
23–27 **Laylat ul-Qadr**
The night of power
on which the Koran
was first revealed

5 Jumada al-Awwal

8 Sha'ban
14–15 **Laylat ul-Barat**
The night when Allah
decides what will
happen in the coming
year to all
His creation

27 **Laylat ul-Isra**
wal Mi'raj
The night journey and
ascent of the Prophet
Muhammad PBUH
Makkah to Jerusalem
and through
the heavens

7 Rajab

20 **The Birthday of**
Fatimah Zarah
The daughter of the
Prophet Muhammad PBUH
and mother of Imam
Husain PUH is called
the leader of women

6 Jumada al-Thani

The Koran

Muslims believe that the **Koran** is **Allah's** final book of guidance, which was revealed to the Prophet Muhammad PBUH for all humankind.

Fatimah is studying her Arabic reading book to learn the words that are written in the Koran.

The language of the Koran

Arabic is the language of the Koran. No matter where they live or what their language is, **Muslims** always read or recite the Koran in Arabic. The words themselves have a special sound. Although it is a very long book, millions of people know it by heart. The Koran has 114 **suras**, or chapters. Each sura is made up of shorter numbered sections. These are the numbers which follow the Koran quotes in this book. The Koran can also be read in 30 sections, one a day for a month, or in seven sections, one for each day of the week. Muslims often read and study translations of the Koran in whatever languages they speak.

" I am learning to read the Koran. First we have to learn the Arabic alphabet. Then we figure out how the words sound. Sometimes they sound like music. That makes it easier to learn.

– *Fatimah* "

ayd ibn Thabit

n **Madinah**, twelve-year-old Zayd ibn Thabit
ffered to fight to defend the Muslim community.
he Prophet PBUH was pleased that Zayd was so
rave, but said that he was too young to fight. Zayd
hought of another way he could help. He could read
nd write very well, and worked hard at learning to
cite the Koran. The Prophet PBUH asked him to
arn Hebrew, so that he could write letters to the
cal Jewish tribes. Later, Zayd learned to read,
rite, and speak the Syriac language. He often wrote
wn parts of the Koran soon after they were
vealed to the Prophet PBUH. When the Prophet
зUH died, Zayd was given the job of collecting all
e parchments and palm leaves on which the Koran
ad been written. With the help of assistants, he
rganized and made copies of everything exactly as
was taught by the Prophet PBUH.

When the Koran is read, listen to it with attention
 silence that you may receive [Allah's] mercy."
oran 7:204)

*After school or
at weekends,
many Muslim
children go to
classes to
learn what the
Koran teaches.*

Hadith

Even though she listens ver[y] carefully, unles[s] Fatimah write[s] down telephon[e] messages, she sometimes ge[ts] them mixed u[p]

> **Sometimes, our teacher lets us play "Pass it On." He whispers a message into one child's ear. Then it is passed one by one around the class. It nearly always comes out wrong. My dad says I'm like that with telephone messages.**
>
> – *Fatimah*

The hadith

The word **hadith** means "saying." The hadith are reports of what the Prophet Muhammad PBUH said. Because he was the living example of Islamic teaching, knowing what he said about how to live is very important to **Muslims**. People who were close to him remembered what he had said and told it to others. Some wrote down what he said. After the Prophet Muhammad PBUH died, people realized the importance of collecting together all the reports of what he had said. That way, the knowledge could be spread widely. The hadith became the second source of all Islamic teaching after the **Koran**. Islamic law is based upon the Koran and people learn about the customs of the Prophet PBUH through the hadith.

These are pages of the Koran—Allah's words. The hadith are reports of what the Prophet Muhammad PBUH said and did.

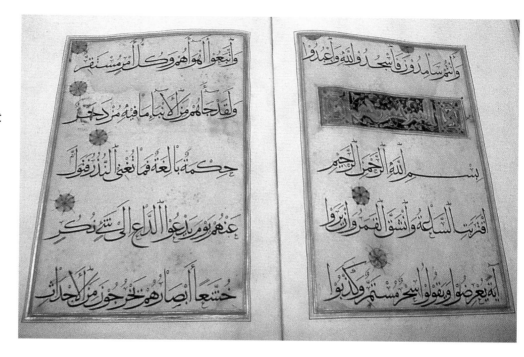

How the hadith were collected and checked

Every hadith that was reported was checked. The person who had told it had to be known to be truthful. What that person said had to match what was known about the Prophet PBUH and Islamic teaching. Because each saying had to be accurate, collecting hadith was very detailed work. If there was any doubt about a hadith's being correct, it was not added to the collections. Many scholars spent their lives doing this work. Some of the most famous collections are:

Sahih al-Bukhari—the collection compiled by Muhammad al-Bukhari

Sahih Muslim—the books of hadith gathered by Abul Husayn Muslim

Al-Kafi—those collected by Muhammad ibn Yaqub Koleini

Beautiful Hadith

Abdullah ibn Amr reported:
The dearest of you to me is the one who is best in conduct.
(Hadith: Bukhari)

Ja'bar reported:
Every good deed is a charity, and it is a good deed to meet people with a cheerful face.
(Hadith: Tirmidhi)

Oqbah ibn A'mer reported:
...All of you are the children of Adam.
...There is no superiority of anyone over another except in faith.
(Hadith: Bayhaqi)

Salah

" When I was really little, I used to try to do salah. My mom says I used to copy her. When she bowed down, I would lie on the prayer mat in front of her. As I got a bit older, she told me to stand beside her and showed me what to do. My granny and grandpa helped me learn the Arabic words of the salah. "
– *Fatimah*

The meanings of the prayer positions

Performing **salah** not only means saying particular words but also making specific movements. Someone even called salah "the Yoga of Islam" because the physical positions help **Muslims** to think about what they are doing and saying to **Allah**. When Muslims pray, they take positions that remind them of how they should behave in front of their Creator.

The obligation to pray

When Muslim children reach the age of seven, their parents must ask them to perform salah. As they reach adolescence, it is up to the young people to make sure they do their salah five times every day. As Allah says in the **Koran**: ". . . And establish regular prayers at the two ends of the day, and at the approaches of the night: for those things that are good remove those that are evil . . ." (Koran 11:114)

While they offer salah, the children turn towards the Ka'bah in Makkah.

Salah positions

Stand upright: *be upright and well-behaved.*

Bow low: *show respect and reverence.*

Kneel down: *show thankfulness.*

Prostrate: *show readiness to do what Allah wants.*

Prayer mats

Some Muslims have a favorite mat that they use to pray on at home. Mats can be made from straw or cotton or be a wool carpet. These mats often have an arch shape at one end. When someone is going to use the mat for salah, he or she lays it in the direction of **Makkah. Shi'ah** Muslims often place a small tablet of clay from Kerbala on the place where their foreheads touch the mat (see pages 18–19).

Hijrah

On the **Hijrah**, in **Muslim** families and communities, the story of the Prophet's move to **Madinah** on the first day of **Muharram** is told.

From the map of Arabia, Fatimah can see how far it is from Makkah to Madinah.

> **Our calendar starts from the day that the Prophet Muhammad PBUH arrived in Madinah to live. My friends think it's funny tha our New Year doesn't often start on January But I've worked out that in the year 2008 a.d., the Islami year of 1430 will start at the beginning of January, too. I'll be grown up then.**
> – *Fatimah*

Leaving Makkah

In the year 622 A.D. the Prophet Muhammad's life was threatened He had been teaching people in **Makkah** about **Allah** and that i was wrong to worship idols and wrong to be greedy and cruel. Many of the people of Makkah were making money from idol worship and they didn't want to lose their businesses. They tried bribe Muhammad PBUH to stop him speaking out, but he would not accept their money.

A Muslim song

Muslims sing "Tala'al badru alaynaa," the song the women and children of Madinah sang to welcome the Prophet PBUH to the safety of their town. Some verses from Tala'al badru alaynaa in English are:

The full moon has arisen
  among us,
We must be thankful
Whenever a messenger calls
  us to Allah.
Oh Messenger, you have come with
A call which must be obeyed.
You have come and honored
  Madinah.
Welcome, oh the best of men.

One night the Prophet PBUH heard that they planned to kill him. His cousin Ali PUH spent that night in the Prophet's house so that it didn't look empty. Meanwhile, Muhammad PBUH and his friend Abu Bakr escaped into the desert. The plotters were furious when they found that he had got away. For a few days the Prophet PBUH and Abu Bakr hid. Then they crisscrossed the desert, all the way north to Madinah. The people of Madinah were very glad that he was coming to live with them. They knew he was a wise and good leader and would help their community.

To show their love for the Prophet PBUH, Muslims visit his mosque in Madinah.

Ahlul-Bayt

Who belongs to the family of the Prophet PBUH?

The Prophet Muhammad PBUH and his wife Khadijah had sons who sadly died while they were still infants. Happily, their beloved daughter Fatimah Zahrah did survive and grew up. Fatimah married Ali PUH, her father's cousin, and had three children—Hasan, Hussain, and Zainab, peace upon them all. Today, their descendants are called Ahlul-Bayt—the people of the house (of the Prophet PBUH). **Allah** told the Prophet's family:

"And be regular in prayer, and give **zakah** and obey Allah and His Messenger. Allah only wants to remove from you all stain, O you members of the household, and to make you pure and spotless." (**Koran** 33:33)

> **My mother is from Ahlul-Bayt—the Prophet's family. She can trace her family back to the Prophet's grandson Hussain PUH. She was born at Kerbala in Iraq, when her family traveled there to visit the tomb of Hussain PUH. It's a responsibility to be from this family and I try to live up to it.**
> – *Hussain*

Hussain's mother shows him old photographs of her family and tells him all about them.

The Prophet's family life

Perhaps because his own sons died, the Prophet Muhammad PBUH especially loved his grandsons, Hasan PUH and Hussain PUH. They looked a lot like their grandfather. He often carried them on his shoulders. Once, when he was speaking to people, the two little boys were toddling around and falling over. He cut short what he was saying, picked them up and sat them with him. He said to the people, "Allah has spoken true—'. . . your possessions and your children are a trial. . .'." (Koran 8:28). (**Hadith**: Tirmidhi, Abu Dawud, and Nisai in Mishkat ul-Masabih)

After his farewell pilgrimage, the Prophet PBUH spoke to his followers at an oasis between **Makkah** and **Madinah**. Before the crowds went their separate ways, he told them that if they wanted to be wise, they should follow the book of Allah—the Koran and "the people of my house." (Hadith: Muslim)

The World Ahlul-Bayt Islamic League is a charitable organization set up by the family of the Prophet PBUH. It provides education and helps people.

Ashura

❝ **Nobody likes bullies and nobody wants them to be in charge of things. The best people to be leaders are the ones who are fair to everyone. Muslims are taught to stick up for what is right and stand up to people who do bad things.** ❞
– *Fatimah*

On the tenth day of **Muharram,** the death of the grandson of the Prophet Muhammad PBUH is remembered. The festival is called Ashura.

Hussain ibn Ali PUH

By the time the Prophet's grandson Hussain PUH had children of his own, the numbers of **Muslims** had grown. Islam had spread very quickly. A man called Yazid had taken power in the Muslim world. He wanted everyone to accept him as the "Leader the Believers." Because he was powerful, many people accepted him as their leader. Hussain PUH and his followers refused, because Yazid was not a good man. Yazid was angry and made up his mind force Hussain PUH to accept him.

The dome and minarets of Imam Hussain's tomb, in Kerbala, Iraq

While they traveled in the desert near Kerbala, Yazid's army stopped Hussain PUH, his family, and his followers from reaching the Euphrates River and getting water. They said that if Hussain PUH would not accept Yazid, they would kill him. Hussain PUH told all the people with him to leave if they wanted to save their lives. None of them did, because they were all loyal to him. In the battle that followed, Hussain's group was greatly outnumbered and many were killed, including Hussain PUH and many of his family. To make sure no one else stood up to Yazid, the remaining family members were sent to him in Damascus.

Traditions

Some Muslim children are taught to remember Hussain PUH and to be thankful whenever they drink water. They learn to say this prayer:

"In the name of **Allah**, most Gracious, most Merciful. Blessings of Allah be upon **Imam** Hussain, his family, and his friends."

In **Shi'ah** Muslim communities, people have parades on Ashura. They act out the story of what happened in Kerbala and feel sad that anyone should treat the family of the Prophet PBUH so badly.

A modern leader of Iraq wanted everyone to bow to his leadership. When they would not, he attacked Kerbala and the tomb of Imam Hussain PUH and killed many people.

Maulid

During the month of Rabi al-Awwal, the birthday of the Prophet Muhammad PBUH—the Maulid an-Nabi—is celebrated.

The Sunnah (tradition) of the Prophet PBUH

Copying the Prophet's example is called following the Sunnah—the customs of the Prophet Muhammad PBUH. The Prophet PBUH always got dressed from the right side first, so **Muslims** do the same. **Allah** tells people, "You have indeed in the Messenger of Allah an excellent example." (**Koran** 33:21)

" **My grandfather tells me lots of stories about the Prophet Muhammad PBUH and how kind he was to people and to animals. The stories teach us that we should try to do what he did.** "
– *Hussain*

Hussain's grandfather can read and understand lots of languages so he translates the stories he knows for Hussain.

Celebrating the Maulid

Many Muslims make this a time when they try to teach others about Islam. Muslim communities hold special events to celebrate the birthday of Prophet Muhammad PBUH. Some Muslim organizations hold a Maulid Dinner every year. The members, their husbands and wives, children, and guests come to the function hall at a big mosque. The young people read **suras** from the Koran and recite poems about the Prophet's life. A well-known person gives a short talk about Islam. Then everyone has an enjoyable meal and talks to their friends.

These Muslims from many different countries have gathered to read about the Prophet Muhammad's PBUH life.

The early life of the Prophet PBUH

Before the Prophet Muhammad PBUH was born in the city of **Makkah,** in the month of Rabi I-Awwal 570 A.D., his father, Abdullah, had been taken ill and had died. His mother, Amina, asked her father-in-law to name her son. The name he chose, Muhammad, means "Praised." As a baby, Muhammad PBUH was sent out of the city to be cared for in the clean, desert air. He grew strong and healthy. When he was about three years old he went to Makkah to live with his mother. She died when he was six. For two years Muhammad PBUH was lovingly cared for by his grandfather, until he too died. He then went to live with his uncle and became one of the favorite children in his large family.

Laylat-ul-Isra wal Mi'raj

This is the rock in Jerusalem from which the Prophet Muhammad PBUH was said to have ascended into the heavens. It is now protected by a beautiful golden domed building.

> **Every day, we offer our salah five times—before dawn, just after midday, in the afternoon, at sunset and at nighttime. When we are at home, my family prays together. While everyone gets ready, I call the adhan in Arabic. Then my dad leads us in the prayer.**
> – *Husain*

Many people try to spend the whole night in prayer in remembrance of Muhammad's night journey and **mi'raj**, or ascent through the heavens.

'Glory to **Allah** who took His servant [Muhammad] for a journey by night from the Sacred Mosque [in Makkah] to the Farthest Mosque [in Jerusalem] whose surroundings We did bless.' (**Koran** 17:1

Pray 50 times a day!

One night, the Prophet Muhammad PBUH lay sleeping near the **Ka'bah** in **Makkah**. The angel **Jibril** (Galbriel) woke him and took him to Jerusalem on the back of a white animal. There they met other prophets, including Ibrahim (Abraham) PUH, Musa (Moses) PUH and Isa (Isaiah) PUH. The Prophet Muhammad PBUH led them in prayer. The angel brought him two jugs. One jug was full of milk, the other was full of wine. Muhammad PBUH chose the milk and refused the wine. The angel said, 'Yo have made the right choice. Wine is forbidden for you and your people, the **Muslims**'.

The Prophet Muhammad PBUH was taken up through the seven heavens into the light of Allah's presence. He was told that Muslims should pray 50 times a day. The Prophet PBUH said that on his way back he met Musa PUH. He asked how many prayers Muhammad PBUH had been ordered to do. When he heard how many, Musa PUH said, "Prayer is serious and people are weak. Go back and ask your Lord to make it less." Muhammad PBUH did, and ten prayers were taken off. The same thing happened several times again with Musa PUH, until only five prayers were left for the whole day. The Prophet PBUH said that he was ashamed to ask for less, and that whoever does the five prayers faithfully will have the reward for 50.

The map shows how far the Prophet Muhammad PBUH traveled from Makkah to Jerusalem and back again, on the night of his journey.

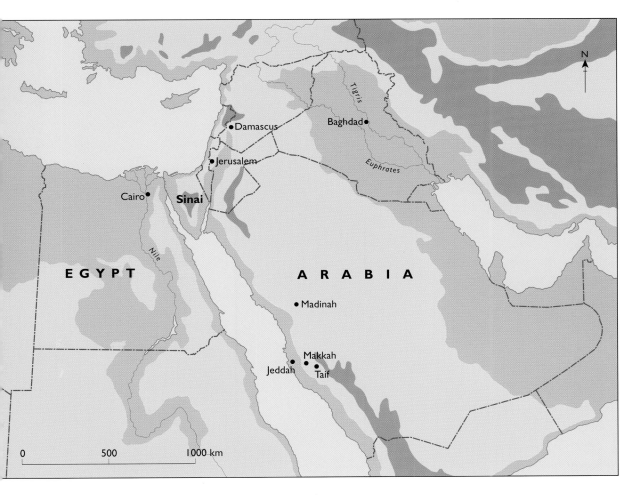

Laylat-ul-Barat

Laylat-ul-Barat is the night of forgiveness, between the 14th and 15th days of the month of Shaban, when **Allah** decides each person's fate and provision for the coming year.

The night of forgiveness

Many **Muslims** believe that on Laylat-ul-Barat Allah decides what will happen to each person during the coming year. They believe Allah rewards their good actions and forgives them when they don't do everything they should. Many people stay up all night thanking Allah for their home, family, and good things. They ask for His forgiveness when they are forgetful about Allah or anything in creation. They ask for Allah's blessings for everyone. Laylat-ul-Barat takes place 15 days before the start of the holy month of **Ramadan**. It is called "the gateway to Ramadan."

> **When I see the good things Allah has given us, I want to thank Allah for fruit, flowers, vegetables, fish, animals, and birds. Scientists are smart but no one can make seeds to grow trees or crops. Allah created the world and everything in it so that we can eat, build homes, and live well.**
> – *Hussain*

Hussain is fascinated that even the bee, one of the smallest creatures, can make the beautifully patterned honeycomb.

This grand building in Jerusalem, with fountains on two sides, supplies fresh drinking water for everyone.

Sharing

To show Allah how thankful they are for all the good things they have, Muslims give food to homeless people and to hostels. They also make long-term gifts that will do a lasting good.

"A man asked the Prophet **PBUH**, 'Which charity is the most excellent?' He replied, 'Water.'"
(**Hadith**: Abu Dawud)

In hot, dry countries, wealthy Muslims had wells dug and water fountains (Waqf fountains) built over them to provide free water for everyone. Many of these also had a drinking trough nearby for animals. Some are still used, hundreds of years later. Other Muslims set up free schools, where anyone who was thirsty for knowledge could learn to read, write, and study the **Koran**. Hospitals, too, were opened to give free treatment to all citizens. Farmers would set aside some trees from their orchards so that people could help themselves to the fruit or the fruit could be sold and the money given in charity.

Ramadan: The Ninth Month (I)

When it's time to break the fast, Hussain really enjoys the taste of that first date.

> **In Ramadan, we get up early, before it starts to get light. We have a meal. I like cornflakes and toast. We drink lots of tea and water. Before the first light of day we stop eating and say, 'I intend to fast today in obedience to Allah Most High.'**
> – *Hussain*

Muslims do not eat or drink from before dawn until sunset for the 29 or 30 days of the month of **Ramadan**. This fasting is called **sawm**.

"Ramadan is the month in which was sent down the **Koran**, as a guide to mankind . . . so every one of you who is present at their home during that month should spend it in fasting . . ." (Koran 2:185)

Fasting

For the first few days of Ramadan, fasting makes people feel a bit tired. When Ramadan occurs in summer, people often take naps when they come home from school or work.

By sunset, everyone is ready to eat. After the **adhan**, the call to prayer, is made, people break their fast by eating a date and drinking water. The Prophet PBUH said: "When you break the fast, do so with dates. If you cannot find any dates, break the fast with water, because it is pure." (**Hadith**: Mishkat al-Masabih)

Fast FM: Keeping Muslims informed

In England, a radio station called Fast FM broadcasts for one month every year. It has programs of Koran readings and lets Muslims know the exact time for starting and breaking the fast each day. During Ramadan, many people stop listening to other radio stations and watching their usual TV programs. They prefer to listen to Fast FM because it helps them concentrate on **Allah.**

A recipe for breaking the fast

Dates fried in butter and served with yogurt

Ingredients:
Dried or fresh dates
Butter
Plain yogurt or cream

Directions:
Cut the dates in half. Remove the stones. Melt some butter in a small pan. Add the dates. Fry slowly for a few minutes until the dates have softened. Serve in individual dishes with the yogurt or other topping.

Hussain's family enjoys inviting people to break the fast with them at home.

Ramadan: The Ninth Month (II)

Fatimah likes to make sure her favorite foods are packed in the Ramadan basket her family takes to the mosque.

Caring for others

Every night during **Ramadan**, some large city mosques hold an evening meal for hundreds of people. The food is sometimes served on trays like airline meals. The community tries to look after poor people, students, travelers, and those who live alone or are separated from their families. They try to make sure that everyone who has fasted during the day has enough to eat. This food is paid for or given to the mosque by Muslims. In Cairo, "Tables of Mercy" are set out in the street by kind people, so that the homeless may eat.

Some evenings in
Ramadan we go to the
mosque in time to pray and to
break our fast. We bring our
food with us and my mom
and dad invite other people
to share what we have
brought.
Fatimah

These Palestinian women are happy to spend every day during Ramadan preparing food for their community to break the fast together each night.

Ramadan in Muslim countries

In countries where most of the people are Muslim, schools don't need to have a lunch break during Ramadan. The students and teachers can go home early. Many banks, businesses, and offices close early to let the fasting workers go home to rest in the afternoon. During the day, most restaurants and cafés are closed until after sunset. In the evening many stores are open because people like to do some shopping at night on their way to and from the mosque.

How long is the fast?

Because the Islamic calendar moves back through the seasons by about 11 days per year (see pages 6–7), the fasting does not always take place during the hottest season of the year, or on the longest summer days. In midsummer, people can be fasting during the daylight hours from about 2:35 A.M. till 9:20 P.M., which is almost 19 hours. In the year 2000, when Ramadan will fall in December, Muslims will fast from about 6:15 A.M. until 4 P.M., which is fewer than 10 hours without food or drink.

Laylat-ul-Qadr

When he was alone in a cave on this mountain, the Prophet Muhammad PBUH learned the first words of Allah's revealed Koran.

The first revelation of the **Koran** came to the Prophet **PBUH** on **Laylat-ul-Qadr**—the night of power. It is a blessed night—one of the last ten nights of **Ramadan**—and **Muslims** try to spend it in prayer.

When you get a new video or computer game, you read the instructions carefully to find out everything it can do, so that you can play it well. Muslims read the Koran to find out Allah's instructions about how to live a good life. Allah created us so He understands what we need to know and do to be happy and successful.

– Hussain

The first revelation

Makkah was a busy, noisy city. The Prophet Muhammad PBUH liked to go to the desert to enjoy the peace. One night, while he was there, the angel **Jibril** spoke to him. "Recite," said Jibril. Muhammad PBUH was too afraid to speak. Three times the angel repeated the words, "Recite, in the name of your Lord who has created, created man out of a germ cell. Recite! And your Lord is the Most Bountiful." (Koran 96:1–3)

Muhammad PBUH said the words back to the angel. He had learned the first words of **Allah's** revealed Koran. For the next 23 years, he learned more and taught it to others.

The night of power in Morocco

In Morocco, Laylat-ul-Qadr is a wonderful night. Towns are brightly lit with thousands of lights strung around the mosques and across the narrow streets. To celebrate, people try to pray in as many mosques as they can between the night and early morning **salah**. Groups of friends walk from mosque to mosque, praying in each place. On the way, they meet other friends and sometimes join up with new groups. The whole town seems to be happily, noisily on the move. Once inside the mosque, the atmosphere is quiet, peaceful, and devoted to prayer and the love of Allah.

The town is brightly lit to attract and welcome everyone on this special night.

Id-ul-Fitr

On Id day, Fatimah doesn't go to school. After going to the mosque, she celebrates with her family and friends.

> **The month of Ramadan is over on the morning after the new moon has been sighted. That is the day of Id-ul-Fitr, the first of the month of Shawal. In our house we get up early ready to go to the mosque. We're lucky because we've got two bathrooms, so everyone can have their shower in time and put on fresh clothes. Our family likes to arrive at the mosque early so that we can find a space inside. People who come later have to pray in the courtyard.**
> – *Fatimah*

The Prophet Muhammad **PBUH** said, "Do not begin the month of fasting until you have seen the crescent of the new moon, and do not finish the month of fasting until you have seen the next new moon. If it is covered with clouds, when you think it should be visible, add an extra day of fasting."
(**Hadith**: Bukhari)

Zakat-ul-Fitr

All adult **Muslims**, men and women, who are the heads of households, have to pay **zakat-ul-Fitr** for themselves and everyone in their family. The amount for each person is the price of a meal. So that every Muslim, however poor, can join in the **Id** day feast, zakat-ul-Fitr ought to be paid before **Id-ul-Fitr**. It can be given directly to the people in need, or it can be given to the mosque **zakah** committee, who will hand it out to the community.

On Id, when people arrive at the mosque, they join in reciting the Id **Takbirs**. They are in Arabic and begin with the words **"Allahu Akbar."**

The Id Takbirs

Allah is great, Allah is great,
Allah is great,
There is no god except Allah,
Allah is great, Allah is great,
To Him belongs all praise,
Allah is the greatest,
All praise is due to Him,
And glory to Allah,
In the evening and the morning,
There is no god except Allah the Unique.

On Id days, the mosques are filled to overflowing and many people make their salah in the outside courtyards.

Sadaqah, Zakah, Khums

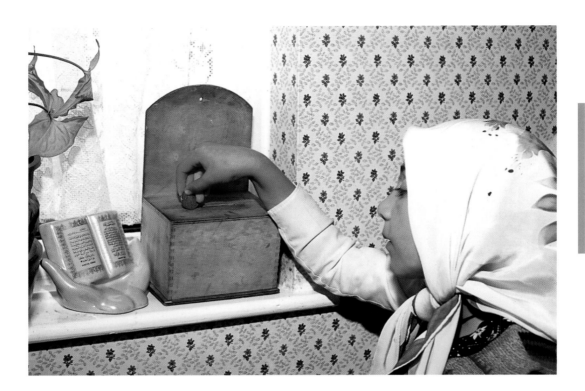

It is good to try to fill the sadaqah box quickly because ther are people a over the wor who need he

> **At home, we keep a charity box for our gifts of sadaqah—charity, near the front door. Before we go out, the family puts some money into it. Even if we only put in a few pennies, the box soon fills up. We use the money to give to charities.**
>
> *– Fatimah*

The Prophet Muhammad PBUH and charitable giving

One day the Prophet Muhammad PBUH was praying in his mosque in **Madinah**. His friends were surprised that as soon as he finished, he walked quickly to his house. Some followed him to ask why he had hurried off. He answered, "I remembered I had some money and wanted to give it to the poor." (**Hadith**: Bukhari)

...akah—collecting and giving

...akah is a welfare tax and the way the **Muslim** ...mmunities make sure that those who can afford it ...lp those in need. Every year, **Sunni** Muslims give ...ay two and a half percent of whatever money, ...ods, and property they have after they have paid ... their own bills. People can pay the money directly ... those in need, or to a zakah committee at their ...osque. If Muslims know about someone who is too ...y to ask for help, they can tell the zakah ...mmittee about that person.

...hums—paid to help the community

...i'ah Muslims pay zakah on nine kinds of wealth. ...ey also pay **khums**—one fifth of what is left after ...ey have paid their bills.

...nd know that whatever thing you gain, a fifth of it ... for Allah, and for the Messenger and for the near ... kin and the orphans and the needy and the ...yfarer. . ." (**Koran** 8:41)

Islamic aid agencies

The Red Crescent is an international Islamic aid agency. It works in war zones and countries which have faced disasters. Muslim Aid and Islamic Relief also help suffering people, whoever and wherever they are. Islamic Relief began with a small donation. Now their volunteers help 4,000 orphans in more than ten countries. Interpal supports widows and orphans in Palestine. Each of them depends on the zakah and **sadaqah** donations of Muslims worldwide.

Islamic relief organizations send out pamphlets to tell people how they can help charities to continue to help others.

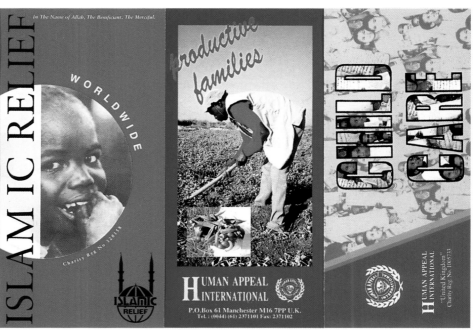

Hajj

The Ka'bah in Makkah is a very old building. Muslims believe it was the first house made for the worship of the One True God. The word Ka'bah means "cube-shaped."

> **My dad told us that he had saved up enough for us to go on a Hajj. I could hardly believe that I would see the Ka'bah and the places where the Prophet PBUH had lived. It would be the journey of a lifetime.**
> – *Hussain*

What is Hajj?

Hajj takes place during set days in the month of Dhul-Hijjah. Every **Muslim** who is healthy and can afford the cost must make the pilgrimage at least once in his or her life. Muslims look forward to completing a Hajj. Pilgrims remember that the **Ka'bah** is the first house built for the worship of the One True God. It was built by the Prophet Ibrahim PUH and his son Ismail PUH over 4,000 years ago. Pilgrims also remember that the Prophet Muhammad PBUH once gave assistance when the Ka'bah was being repaired. Pilgrims walk around the Ka'bah seven times, praying to **Allah.** Ismail's mother, Hajar, searched for water for her baby son by hurrying between two hills, and pilgrims follow in her footsteps. Then, at the plain of Arafat, pilgrims think about what the Prophet PBUH said in his last speech and ask Allah for His forgiveness. Pilgrims then throw stones at three pillars at **Mina** in memory of Ismail PUH, who threw stones at the devils who wanted him to disobey his father Ibrahim PUH.

Then when you pour down from Arafat, remember Allah at the holy place and celebrate His praises."
(**Koran** 2:198)

Crowds of pilgrims gather at Arafat where the Prophet Muhammad PBUH gave his last speech.

Teaching Muslims how to live

The millions of Muslims who go each year to Hajj are of every color and from every nation on earth. Each person is a part of the worldwide community of Muslims. Being together on Hajj teaches them about loving their neighbors. Traveling together is a lesson for everyone in being kind and patient.

A Hajj Diary

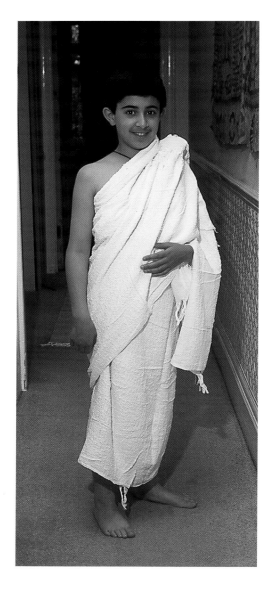

Hussain made all his preparations and put on his pilgrim clothes, "Ihram," before setting off on the Hajj.

> **My whole family came to see us off. At the check-in, big Hajj stickers were put on our luggage. Everyone on our plane seemed to be a Muslim on the way to Hajj. I took a notebook and wrote down everything we did.**
> *– Hussain*

Arriving in Arabia

Our flight to Jeddah lasted six hours. Planes were arriving from all over the world. We saw **Muslims** from Indonesia, Senegal and Great Britain. People were speaking in lots of different languages, but everyone greeted us in Arabic, saying "peace be wit you." It was as if we all knew one another. Everyone got on buses and set off for **Makkah**. It was very hot.

Changing into Ihram

Ten miles away from Makkah, the bus stopped and everyone who had not yet prepared themselves for **Ihram**, the state of purity and readiness for **Hajj**, got out. They showered and changed into pilgrim clothes. All the men were dressed in two large white cloths. Many of the women wore white dresses and had scarves on their heads.

Entering Makkah and seeing the Ka'bah

I'll never forget seeing the **Ka'bah** for the first time. I didn't know it would be so big, yet it looked as though it could rise up out of the huge crowds. We thanked **Allah** for blessing us with this visit to His House. Then we walked around the Ka'bah. It took a long time and it seemed as though everyone in the world was there with us. Then we sat in the mosque and drank **Zamzam** water, which Allah had provided for Ismail PUH and Hajar and all the pilgrims for thousands of years up to today.

Mina and Arafat

On the days of Hajj, all the pilgrims went out of Makkah to **Mina** and Arafat, where we prayed for ourselves, our family, and friends. The next day was **Id**. We stoned the pillars and visited the Ka'bah. Everyone was very tired. The time for Ihram was over and we spent the next two days at Mina. I made friends with a German boy called Hasan. My mom said we made a good pair—"Hasan and Hussain," like the grandsons of the Prophet PBUH.

Every year during the Hajj, more than 2 million Muslims from all over the world gather to pray by the Ka'bah.

Id-ul-Adha

Muslims sacrifice a sheep or a goat on the tenth day of **Dhul-Hijjah** to remember what happened to the Prophet Ibrahim PUH and his son Ismail PUH, and how they were willing to obey **Allah**.

Pilgrims often bring home Zamzam water from Makkah, to share its blessings with family and friends.

" Last year my uncle and his family went on Hajj. They brought back Zamzam water for us. I asked them lots of questions about Hajj. My aunt liked being near the Ka'bah. My cousins liked sleeping in the big tents at Mina and my uncle said everything about Hajj made him want to go again. "
— *Fatimah*

What happens on Id-ul-Adha

Early in the morning of **Id-ul-Adha**, Muslims everywhere shower and put on their best clothes. They set off to the largest mosques in their areas. The Id prayer is an extra prayer between early morning and afternoon. The **Imam** leads the people in prayer. Then he talks about the meaning and importance of **Id**. He often reminds everyone about the sense of community among people during the **Hajj**. He encourages Muslims to keep this feeling for the whole year.

Many Islamic relief organizations give meat to Muslims in need all over the world, so that they can all join in the feast which is held on Id-ul-Adha.

The Prophet Ibrahim PUH and his son Ismail PUH

Ibrahim PUH was an old man when he prayed, "O my Lord! Grant me a righteous son!" Allah answered his prayer and his son Ismail PUH was born. When he grew up and was old enough to work alongside his father, Ibrahim PUH dreamed that he should sacrifice his son. He told Ismail PUH about his dream and asked him what he thought. His son answered, "O my father, do as you are commanded. You will find me, if Allah so wills, one of the steadfast." They were both willing to obey what they thought Allah wanted and got ready to sacrifice Ismail PUH. But Allah spoke to them, saying, "O Ibrahim, you have already fulfilled the purpose of the dream." Because they had been so obedient, Allah gave them a sheep to sacrifice instead. (Koranic quotes taken from 37:100–105.)

On Id day these Muslims have come to the mosque to hear their Imam, Sheikh Nazim, teach about respect for all of Allah's creation.

Jumu'ah

It's time for prayer and Hussain is calling the adhan to let everyone know "Come to prayer; come to success."

Coming together

Every Friday, local **Muslims** come together for **Jumu'ah**. Twice a year, Muslim communities gather for **Id**, and once in each Muslim's life he or she has the chance on **Hajj** to be with Muslims from all over the world.

> **Every Friday I go with my family to Salat-ul-Jumu'ah—the Friday prayers at the main mosque. I look forward to it because I know I will meet all my friends after the prayers. At our mosque, there is a room for babies and small children to play, so that they don't disturb the people who want to listen and pray.**
> *– Hussain*

On Friday, people leave work in time to get to the mosque.

) you who believe! When the
ll to prayer is proclaimed on
riday (the day of assembly)
asten earnestly to the
:membrance of **Allah** and leave
f business . . . And when the
rayer is finished, then may you
isperse throughout the land and
:ek the bounty of Allah: and
:member Allah frequently, that
ou may prosper." (**Koran**
2:9–10)

ımu'ah salah

ecause Friday is the day that
Iuslims meet together and pray, it is the
ommunity's weekly celebration. On Friday, after
nowering, people put on fresh clothes to go to the
osque. However, it is not a holiday. In the
orning, up to noon, most people are at work or
chool as usual. During their lunch break, they go to
le mosque. Part of the purpose of Salat-ul-Jumu'ah
to listen to the talk by the **Imam**. He tells the
eople important things about Islamic events and
ves them advice about everyday life. The Imam
ies to make his talk interesting to young people
id adults.

The mosque

There are hundreds of mosques in the United States. Most universities and even some hospitals have a place where the Muslims can come together to perform Salat-ul-Jumu'ah. Muslims in Europe save up to build mosques big enough to hold all of their community for festivals and Friday prayers. A mosque can be a real community center for people.

Glossary

Adhan call to prayer. A Mu'adhin is the person who makes the call to prayer.

al-Kafi the title of the books of Hadith, put together by Muhammad ibn-Yaqub Kolieni, a Shi'ah scholar.

Allah the Islamic name for the One True God in the Arabic language.

Allahu Akbar "Allah is Most Great."

Dhul-Hijjah the month of the Hajj, the last month of the Islamic year.

fajr (Salat-ul-Fajr) the dawn salah, which may be performed from dawn until just before sunrise.

hadith the sayings of the Prophet Muhammad PBUH, as reported by his friends, children, and household. These are an important source of Islamic law.

Hajj the annual pilgrimage to Makkah, which each Muslim must undertake at least once in a lifetime, if he or she has the health and wealth.

Hijrah "departure"; the emigration, or departure, of the Prophet Muhammad PBUH from Makkah to Madinah in 622 A.D. The Islamic calendar starts with this event.

Id "happiness"; a religious holiday, a feast to thank Allah and celebrate a happy occasion.

Id-ul-Adha celebration of the sacrifice, to remember how obedient the Prophets Ibrahim and Isma'il (peace be upon them) were to Allah.

Id-ul-Fitr celebration of breaking the fast on the day after Ramadan ends, which is also the first day of Shawal, the tenth Islamic month.

Ihram the state that Muslims must be in to perform Hajj. Also the name of the two plain, white, unsewn cloths worn by male pilgrims to show the equality and purity of pilgrims.

Imam "leader"; a man who leads Muslims together in prayer.

Jibril Gabriel the angel, who delivered Allah's messages to His Prophets.

jumu'ah (Salat-ul-Jumu'ah) the weekly community salah and talk, shortly after midday on Fridays.

Ka'bah a cube-shaped building in the center of the grand mosque in Makkah; the first house built for the worship of Allah, the One True God.

khums a contribution made by Shi'ah Muslims of one-fifth of their extra income every year.

Koran the Divine Book, revealed to Prophet Muhammad PBUH. Allah's final revelation to mankind.

Laylat-ul-Qadr the night of power, when the first revelation of the Koran was made to Prophet Muhammad PBUH.

Madinah "city"; the City of the Prophet, the name given to the place where Muhammad PBUH went to live. This is also sometimes spelled Medina.

Makkah the city where Prophet Muhammad PBUH was born and where the Ka'bah is located. This is also sometimes spelled Mecca.

Mina the place near Makkah where pilgrims stay on the tenth, eleventh, and twelfth of Duhl-Hijjah and perform some of the activities of the Hajj.

mi'raj the ascent through the heavens of Prophet Muhammad PBUH.

Muharram the first month in the Islamic calendar, which is calculated from the time the Prophet PBUH moved to Madinah.

Muslim someone who claims to have accepted Islam by saying the shahadah.

PBUH "peace and blessings of Allah upon him"; the words said in Arabic by Muslims every time the Prophet Muhammad PBUH is mentioned.

PUH "peace be upon him"; the words said in Arabic by Muslims every time prophets and the twelve Shi'ah Imams are mentioned.

Ramadan the ninth month of the Islamic calendar, when Muslims fast from just before dawn until sunset, as ordered by Allah in the Koran.

sadaqah a voluntary payment or good action for charity.

salah communication with and worship of Allah, taught by the Prophet Muhammad PBUH and recited in the Arabic language. Performing the salah five daily times is fixed by Allah.

sawm fasting from just before dawn until sunset; not eating any food or drink (including water).

shahadah a declaration of faith: "There is no god except Allah, Muhammad is the Messenger of Allah."

Shi'ah "followers"; Muslims who believe that Ali PUH should have been the successor of the Prophet Muhammad PBUH.

Sunni Muslims who accept that Abu Bakr, Umar, Uthman, and Ali (may Allah be pleased with them) were the rightful leaders of the Muslims after the Prophet Muhammad PBUH.

sura a division of the Koran (there are 114 in all).

Takbir saying "Allahu Akbar!" during Salah, Id, and other occasions.

zakah every year Muslims have to pay a set proportion of their wealth to help others.

zakat-ul-Fitr paying money for the benefit of others at the end of Ramadan.

Zamzam the well near the Ka'bah in Makkah, where water first sprang in answer to Hajar's search and prayers.

More Books to Read

Islam. Khadijah Knight; Thomson
Learning, 1995.

Understanding Religions: Food and Fasting.
Deidre Burke, Wayland (Publishers) Ltd.,
1992.

*Understanding Religions: Pilgrimages and
Journeys.* Katherine Prior, Wayland
(Publishers) Ltd., 1992.

A Closer Look

This picture shows pilgrims gathering at Arafat, where the Prophet Muhammad PBUH gave his last speech. In this speech he told Muslims that whatever their race or color, everyone is equal before Allah. Each one of them should be trustworthy and responsible for his or her own actions. They should not oppress people or charge interest on any loan. Women should be treated fairly. He reminded them of their duties as Muslims—saying the salah five times daily, fasting in Ramadan, completing their Hajj, paying Zakah, and believing in the one true God. He asked if he had been clearly understood and the people answered "Yes."

Index